Gratitude 101 Journal

101 Days of Unique Prompts, Positive Affirmations, and Inspirational Quotes for Happiness

BY LYNN LOK-PAYNE

WELLMINDED
MEDIA

This gratitude journal belongs to:

_____

Library of Congress Control Number: 2024904533

Blue Cover ISBN: 9798990245808 (hardcover), 9798990245815 (paperback)
Green Cover ISBN: 9798990245822 (hardcover), 9798990245839 (paperback)
Orange Cover ISBN: 9798990245846 (hardcover), 9798990245853 (paperback)
Published by WellMinded Media
3941 Park Drive, Ste 20-559
El Dorado Hills, CA 95762

www.LynnLokPayne.com
Cover Design: Lynn Lok-Payne, Book Design: McKenna Payne
Printed in The United States of America

TO MY DAUGHTER
WHO TAUGHT ME THE VALUE
OF GRATITUDE BY ALWAYS FINDING JOY
IN SIMPLE, ORDINARY MOMENTS.

TO MY PARENTS AND SISTER
WHO ALWAYS BELIEVED IN ME.
I AM SO GRATEFUL FOR ALL OF YOU!

Introduction

Gratitude is a practice and a mindset. The more we search for it, the more things to appreciate appear. Gradually, gratitude will become a daily habit.

Even when things don't go as planned, we can still seek gratitude. I'm not saying that it is always easy, because it's not. But when we can find something, anything, to be grateful for, like a sunrise or a meal, we can lessen our suffering, even if it's just a little.

I've found that my greatest joys come from the small, everyday moments. In the most difficult times of my life, gratitude was my saving grace and helped me to discover happiness again.

This book offers a simple and quick way to boost gratitude with the help of daily prompts. It's designed to inspire, encourage, and motivate us to seek gratitude, especially in the little things.

Find a few moments each day to reflect and give thanks for the good things in life. Once we shift our perspective, we realize there truly is much to be thankful for.

Pause each day to express gratitude. Embracing gratitude is one of the best gifts you can give yourself!

Maximize the Benefits

- Schedule time to journal
- Find a quiet space away from distractions
- Take a few deep breaths to center yourself
- Read the quote for inspiration
- Say the affirmation out loud
- Use the prompts to encourage appreciation for life's small moments
- If you write earlier in the day, you can review your writing before bed to reinforce the message
- There's no pressure so don't worry if you miss a day; go at your own pace
- Most of all, enjoy the process

*Acknowledging the good
that you already have in your life
is the foundation for all abundance.*

— ECKHART TOLLE

Start each day with a positive thought and a grateful heart.

— ROY T. BENNETT

I give thanks for today.

Today I seek gratitude by...

_____

_____

_____

_____

I look forward to...

_____

_____

_____

_____

One thing I am grateful for is...

_____

_____

_____

_____

Date: _____

Creating an attitude of gratitude is the biggest key to living a well-lived life!

— LYNN LOK-PAYNE

I am grateful.

I find gratitude within me when I...

_____

_____

_____

_____

It makes me happy when...

_____

_____

_____

_____

The good thing about my life is...

_____

_____

_____

_____

Date: _____

INSPIRATIONAL QUOTE

Gratitude is the healthiest of all human emotions. The more you express gratitude for what you have, the more likely you will have even more to express gratitude for.

— ZIG ZIGLAR

I will show appreciation today.

Being grateful for... gives me more to appreciate.

_____

_____

_____

_____

I find joy through...

_____

_____

_____

_____

The thing I enjoy most is...

_____

_____

_____

_____

Date: _____

*There are only two ways to live your life.
One is as though nothing is a miracle. The
other is as though everything is a miracle.*

— ALBERT EINSTEIN

I will look for the good.

I cultivate gratitude through...

_____

_____

_____

_____

Today, I will redirect my focus toward...

_____

_____

_____

_____

What I like most about me is...

_____

_____

_____

_____

Date: _____

Appreciate the present moment because this is where all possibilities exist.

— LYNN LOK-PAYNE

Today is full of potential.

I bring appreciation into my life by...

_____

_____

_____

_____

My source of inspiration is...

_____

_____

_____

_____

One thing I truly appreciate is...

_____

_____

_____

_____

Date: _____

Gratitude also opens your eyes to the limitless potential of the universe, while dissatisfaction closes your eyes to it.

— STEPHEN RICHARDS

The world is full of possibilities.

I attract gratitude by doing...

_____

_____

_____

_____

The thing that inspires me most is...

_____

_____

_____

_____

I am lucky to have in my life...

_____

_____

_____

_____

Date: _____

The struggle ends when gratitude begins.

— NEALE DONALD WALSCH

I am thankful for what I have.

I am thankful for...

_____

_____

_____

_____

I tap into the power of gratitude by...

_____

_____

_____

_____

My favorite part about my life is...

_____

_____

_____

_____

Date: _____

Journaling grants me the opportunity to discover everything I am grateful for in my life.

— LYNN LOK-PAYNE

I purposely seek gratitude.

My goal for today is to discover gratitude through...

_____

_____

_____

_____

It brightens my day when...

_____

_____

_____

_____

The thing that brings me the most joy is...

_____

_____

_____

_____

Date: _____

Gratitude can transform any situation. It alters your vibration, moving you from negative energy to positive. It's the quickest, easiest, most powerful way to effect change in your life–this I know for sure.

— OPRAH WINFREY

Gratitude changes everything.

Appreciation blossoms inside me when I...

_____

_____

_____

_____

I find happiness in...

_____

_____

_____

I reveal my greatest strength when I...

_____

_____

_____

_____

Date: _____

*The number one joy indicator,
the one thing that will predict
whether someone feels joy in their life
or not, is the practice of gratitude.*

— JOHN O'LEARY

Gratitude is the easiest path to joy.

Being grateful for... brings more joy to me.

_____

_____

_____

_____

I am excited for...

_____

_____

_____

_____

I feel fortunate to have...

_____

_____

_____

_____

Date: _____

As we express our gratitude, we must never forget that the highest appreciation is not to utter words, but to live by them.

— JOHN F. KENNEDY

I strive to live in gratitude.

My focus for today is to explore gratitude through...

_____

_____

_____

_____

I find fulfillment in...

_____

_____

_____

_____

I am honored to have in my life...

_____

_____

_____

_____

Date: _____

Each morning I give thanks for the gift, the opportunity, to live another day.

— LYNN LOK-PAYNE

I am grateful for what I have.

I build appreciation when I...

_____

_____

_____

_____

Today I shift my attention to...

_____

_____

_____

The things that are working out for me are...

_____

_____

_____

_____

Date: _____

*When you are grateful, fear disappears
and abundance appears.*

— TONY ROBBINS

TODAY'S AFFIRMATION

Gratitude is the key to abundance.

I build appreciation when I...

_____

_____

_____

_____

The thing that truly ignites my inspiration is...

_____

_____

_____

I am most passionate about...

_____

_____

_____

_____

Date: _____

*Make gratitude a daily practice
by feeling, showing, and embodying it.
Cultivating gratitude brings meaning
to life and magnifies your joy, peace,
contentment, and love.*

— LYNN LOK-PAYNE

I take time today to be thankful.

I am committed to discover appreciation in...

_____

_____

_____

_____

I display my thanks through...

_____

_____

_____

_____

What I love most about myself is...

_____

_____

_____

_____

Date: _____

It's up to us to choose contentment and thankfulness now–and to stop imagining that we have to have everything perfect before we'll be happy.

— JOANNA GAINES

Gratitude is a path to happiness.

Gratitude appears when I...

_____

_____

_____

_____

I leverage the power of gratitude by...

_____

_____

_____

_____

I am privileged to have...

_____

_____

_____

_____

Date: _____

Living in a state of gratitude is the gateway to grace.

— ARIANNA HUFFINGTON

Today I live in gratitude.

I spot gratitude whenever I...

_____

_____

_____

_____

It puts a smile on my face when...

_____

_____

_____

This individual is special to me because...

_____

_____

_____

_____

Date: _____

*In ordinary life we hardly realize
that we receive a great deal more
than we give, and that it is only with
gratitude that life becomes rich.*

— DEITRICH BONHOEFFER

I'm grateful for simple moments.

I nurture appreciation through...

_____

_____

_____

_____

Whenever..., I feel a boost of positivity.

_____

_____

_____

One thing going right in my life is...

_____

_____

_____

_____

Date: _____

Gratitude can transform common days into thanksgivings, turn routine jobs into joy, and change ordinary opportunities into blessings.

— WILLIAM ARTHUR WARD

TODAY'S AFFIRMATION

Gratitude helps me to be present.

My focus is on searching for thankfulness in...

_____

_____

_____

_____

It makes me feel good when...

_____

_____

_____

I find happiness in doing...

_____

_____

_____

_____

Date: _____

If you concentrate on finding whatever is good in every situation, you will discover that your life will suddenly be filled with gratitude, a feeling that nurtures the soul.

— HAROLD KUSHNER

Gratitude magnifies my joy.

I search to find the good by...

_____

_____

_____

_____

Happiness for me is...

_____

_____

_____

I tap into my true power when I...

_____

_____

_____

_____

Date: _____

Let gratitude be the pillow upon which you kneel to say your nightly prayer. And let faith be the bridge you build to overcome evil and welcome good.

— MAYA ANGELOU

Gratitude is a bridge to goodness.

Appreciation is increased when I...

_____

_____

_____

_____

More opportunities arise when I...

_____

_____

_____

_____

I consider myself lucky to have in my life...

_____

_____

_____

_____

Date: _____

Appreciating what you have is the secret to feeling fulfilled and content, as it helps you recognize you already have enough.

— LYNN LOK-PAYNE

TODAY'S AFFIRMATION

I consciously seek gratitude.

By doing..., I can attract gratitude.

_____

_____

_____

_____

Fulfillment helps me to...

_____

_____

_____

I cherish my relationship with... because...

_____

_____

_____

_____

Date: _____

Gratitude opens the door to the power, the wisdom, the creativity of the universe. You open the door through gratitude.

— DEEPAK CHOPRA

I embrace gratitude.

Focusing on... increases my gratitude.

_____

_____

_____

_____

Today, my choice is to...

_____

_____

_____

_____

The universe is helping me by...

_____

_____

_____

_____

Date: _____

Feeling grateful or appreciative of someone or something in your life actually attracts more of the things that you appreciate and value into your life.

— CHRISTIANE NORTHRUP

Gratitude flows easily through me.

I'm actively looking for reasons to be thankful for...

_____

_____

_____

_____

I direct my awareness to...

_____

_____

_____

_____

I treasure the growth in my relationship with...

_____

_____

_____

_____

Date: _____

I've found in my life that the easiest way to increase my joy is to religiously practice gratitude until I'm a gratitude machine!

— RHONDA BYRNE

Gratitude attracts more gratitude.

My gratitude is sparked by...

_____

_____

_____

_____

I am filled with gratitude when...

_____

_____

_____

_____

I absolutely love to...

_____

_____

_____

_____

Date: _____

Strive to find things to be thankful for,
and just look for the good in who you are.

— BETHANY HAMILTON

I am thankful for me!

I experience appreciation through...

_____

_____

_____

_____

My way of showing appreciation is by...

_____

_____

_____

_____

One of the best things about my personality is...

_____

_____

_____

_____

Date: _____

If the world had more people like you it would be a better place. You do make a difference.

— CATHERINE PULSIFER

I am thankful for you!

By..., I foster gratitude in my life.

_____

_____

_____

_____

It lifts my spirits when...

_____

_____

_____

_____

This person has a special place in my heart because...

_____

_____

_____

_____

Date: _____

*Always remember people
who have helped you along the way,
and don't forget to lift someone up.*

— ROY T. BENNETT

I appreciate the help of others.

When I accept help, I discover...

_____

_____

_____

_____

The root of my happiness is...

_____

_____

_____

_____

I value my connection with... because...

_____

_____

_____

_____

Date: _____

Silent gratitude isn't very much use to anyone.

— GERTRUDE STEIN

I say thank you daily.

When I..., I identify something to be grateful for.

_____

_____

_____

_____

I feel complete when...

_____

_____

_____

It's an honor to know...

_____

_____

_____

_____

Date: _____

*Let us be grateful to the people
who make us happy; they are
the charming gardeners
who make our souls blossom.*

— MARCEL PROUST

Gratitude fills my heart.

I appreciate the people in my life today, including...

_____

_____

_____

_____

I am inspired by...

_____

_____

_____

_____

I am blessed to have... in my life.

_____

_____

_____

_____

Date: _____

We must find time to stop and thank the people who make a difference in our lives.

— JOHN F. KENNEDY

I make an effort to say thank you.

Today, I strive to find appreciation in...

_____

_____

_____

_____

I express gratitude by doing...

_____

_____

_____

I made a positive impact today by...

_____

_____

_____

_____

Date: _____

Let others know their significance.
Your impact lies in making others feel
appreciated, seen, heard, and understood.

— LYNN LOK-PAYNE

I appreciate the people in my life.

Thankfulness runs through me when I...

_____

_____

_____

_____

I get inspired by...

_____

_____

_____

_____

I am a better person today because I met...

_____

_____

_____

_____

Date: _____

*Appreciation is a wonderful thing.
It makes what is excellent in others
belong to us as well.*

— VOLTAIRE

I appreciate you and your talents.

I create gratitude when I...

_____

_____

_____

_____

My optimism shines through...

_____

_____

_____

_____

I feel blessed to have...

_____

_____

_____

_____

Date: _____

I don't have to chase extraordinary moments to find happiness–it's right in front of me if I'm paying attention and practicing gratitude.

— BRENÉ BROWN

Gratitude lives within me.

I recognize something to be grateful for through...

_____

_____

_____

_____

Whenever I..., I feel uplifted.

_____

_____

_____

_____

Positive outcomes come to me when I focus on...

_____

_____

_____

_____

Date: _____

There is always, always, always something to be thankful for.

— UNKNOWN

Gratitude is right here, right now.

I can find gratitude in this moment because...

_____

_____

_____

_____

I feel great when I...

_____

_____

_____

_____

Today, I will... because it makes me happy.

_____

_____

_____

_____

Date: _____

INSPIRATIONAL QUOTE

*We can only be said to be alive
in those moments when our hearts
are conscious of our treasures.*

— THORNTON WILDER

I'm thankful for my treasures.

Through..., I cultivate appreciation.

_____

_____

_____

_____

Today, I turn my focus to...

_____

_____

_____

_____

I shine the most when...

_____

_____

_____

_____

Date: _____

Enjoy the little things, for one day you may look back and realize they were the big things.

— ROBERT BRAULT

I give thanks for the little things.

I feel grateful when...

_____

_____

_____

_____

I harness the power of gratitude through...

_____

_____

_____

I am blessed with...

_____

_____

_____

_____

Date: _____

*Gratitude helps you to grow and expand;
gratitude brings joy and laughter
into your life and into the lives
of all those around you.*

— EILEEN CADDY

Gratitude helps me to evolve.

My objective today is to find thankfulness by...

_____

_____

_____

_____

It fills me with happiness when...

_____

_____

_____

When I..., I unleash my true power.

_____

_____

_____

_____

Date: _____

Focus on the good you have,
not the lack of it, because whatever
gets your attention will increase the energy
of gratitude. That's how joy rises.

— UNKNOWN

I focus on the good, not the lack.

I am really thankful for...

_____

_____

_____

_____

My source of joy is...

_____

_____

_____

I am lucky to possess the skill of...

_____

_____

_____

_____

Date: _____

Appreciation is paying it forward to yourself.

— LYNN LOK-PAYNE

Gratitude is my greatest gift.

I find something to be thankful for when I...

_____

_____

_____

_____

Fulfillment leads me to...

_____

_____

_____

_____

Life is wonderful because I choose to...

_____

_____

_____

_____

Date: _____

My body is a garden rooted in gratitude.
Thank you is the biggest poem
I've got inside of me.

— SABRINA BENAIM

Gratitude makes me kinder.

I feel most grateful whenever I...

_____

_____

_____

_____

I draw inspiration from...

_____

_____

_____

_____

When I..., life gets better and better.

_____

_____

_____

_____

Date: _____

It's not what you say to everyone else that determines your life; it's what you whisper to yourself that has the greatest power.

— UNKNOWN

My self-talk is built on gratitude.

By thinking..., I attract appreciation.

_____

_____

_____

_____

I tap into the strength of gratitude by...

_____

_____

_____

_____

Nothing brings me more joy than...

_____

_____

_____

_____

Date: _____

Gratitude makes sense of our past, brings peace for today, and creates a vision for tomorrow.

— MELODY BEATTIE

Gratitude is the core of my being.

Today, I am dedicated to exploring gratitude by...

_____

_____

_____

_____

I radiate optimism when...

_____

_____

_____

_____

I feel most empowered when...

_____

_____

_____

_____

Date: _____

*By practicing gratitude, we can actually
wire our brains to help us build resilience.*

— CHRISTINA COSTA

I am a gratitude builder.

Thankfulness appears through...

_____

_____

_____

_____

I am looking forward to...

_____

_____

_____

Today, I will appreciate...

_____

_____

_____

_____

Date: _____

*He is a wise man who does not grieve
for the things which he has not,
but rejoices for those which he has.*

— EPICTETUS

I'm thankful for what I receive.

My mission for today is to find appreciation for...

_____

_____

_____

_____

This small blessing inspired me to...

_____

_____

_____

_____

Life becomes amazing when I...

_____

_____

_____

_____

Date: _____

*It's a funny thing about life,
once you begin to take note of the things
you are grateful for, you begin to lose sight
of the things that you lack.*

— GERMANY KENT

Gratitude lowers scarcity mindset.

I appreciate...

_____

_____

_____

_____

What keeps me going is...

_____

_____

_____

I experience a better life when I...

_____

_____

_____

_____

Date: _____

*Be thankful for what you have;
you'll end up having more. If you
concentrate on what you don't have,
you will never, ever have enough.*

— OPRAH WINFREY

I appreciate the things I have.

By doing..., I allow gratitude to flow toward me.

_____

_____

_____

_____

I feel uplifted when...

_____

_____

_____

_____

One of my favorite things is...

_____

_____

_____

_____

Date: _____

*Prioritizing gratitude
paves the way for success.*

— LYNN LOK-PAYNE

Today's #1 priority is gratitude.

Today, I will find appreciation by doing...

_____

_____

_____

_____

My happiness stems from...

_____

_____

_____

_____

What I love most is...

_____

_____

_____

_____

Date: _____

*Gratitude is a posture of your heart.
I believe that it has been a gatekeeper
in my life and has brought on
so many blessings.*

— AMANDA KLOOTS

I'm thankful for all my blessings.

Gratitude becomes a blessing when I choose to do...

_____

_____

_____

_____

I feel fulfilled when...

_____

_____

_____

_____

When... happens, I reveal my full potential.

_____

_____

_____

_____

Date: _____

Something so simple, but it's important to take the time out from living and just appreciate what you've got right in front of you.

— L.A. FIORE

I cherish this present moment.

I am grateful for this moment because...

_____

_____

_____

_____

By..., more opportunities present themselves.

_____

_____

_____

_____

It's a gift to have...

_____

_____

_____

_____

Date: _____

The unthankful heart discovers no mercies; but the thankful heart will find, in every hour, some heavenly blessings.

— HENRY WARD BEECHER

Blessings are all around me!

I find something to be thankful for when I...

_____

_____

_____

_____

When I feel ungrateful, I shift my focus to...

_____

_____

_____

I feel blessed when...

_____

_____

_____

_____

Date: _____

Sometimes we spend so much time and energy thinking about where we want to go that we don't notice where we happen to be.

— DAN GUTMAN

Today I will enjoy the journey.

When I..., I highlight the gratitude in my life.

_____

_____

_____

_____

I feel optimistic when...

_____

_____

_____

I am grateful for my friendship with...

_____

_____

_____

_____

Date: _____

Develop an attitude of gratitude, and give thanks for everything that happens to you, knowing that every step forward is a step toward achieving something bigger and better than your current situation.

— BRIAN TRACY

TODAY'S AFFIRMATION

I step into gratitude.

My life is filled with thankfulness when I...

_____

_____

_____

_____

Today's intention is...

_____

_____

_____

It's a wonderful life because...

_____

_____

_____

_____

Date: _____

Be thankful for everything that happens in your life; it's all an experience.

— ROY T. BENNETT

Gratitude brings opportunities.

I am thankful for everything, including...

_____

_____

_____

_____

I receive joy when I...

_____

_____

_____

_____

What I enjoy above all else is...

_____

_____

_____

_____

Date: _____

INSPIRATIONAL QUOTE

I've discovered that the more you appreciate, the more you will receive.

— LYNN LOK-PAYNE

Thankful for what I've been given.

I nurture appreciation by doing...

_____

_____

_____

_____

I feel grateful whenever I...

_____

_____

_____

When it comes to..., I consider myself blessed.

_____

_____

_____

_____

Date: _____

*She could go on asking herself
why roses had thorns or she could
be thankful that thorns had roses.*

— ELLA GRIFFIN

Today I'll look for life's beauty.

I attract thankfulness into my life when I...

_____

_____

_____

_____

I discover happiness in...

_____

_____

_____

_____

Something I am grateful for is...

_____

_____

_____

_____

Date: _____

INSPIRATIONAL QUOTE

The more grateful I am,
the more beauty I see.

— MARY DAVIS

Gratitude expands life's wonders.

Today's intention is to discover gratitude through...

_____

_____

_____

_____

I am fulfilled by...

_____

_____

_____

_____

My connection with... makes me happy.

_____

_____

_____

_____

Date: _____

When gratitude becomes an essential foundation in our lives, miracles start to appear everywhere.

— EMMANUEL DAGHER

Thankfulness leads to a better life.

I feel thankful for...

_____

_____

_____

_____

My gratitude power lies in me doing...

_____

_____

_____

_____

Good things happen to me when I...

_____

_____

_____

_____

Date: _____

Sometimes your joy is the source of your smile, but sometimes your smile can be the source of your joy.

— THICH NHAT HANH

Smiling is joy shining through.

My appreciation is increased through...

_____

_____

_____

_____

It brings me joy when...

_____

_____

_____

I shine brightest when...

_____

_____

_____

_____

Date: _____

Love wholeheartedly, be surprised, give thanks and praise–then you will discover the fullness of your life.

— DAVID STEINDL-RAST

Gratitude makes life better.

Whenever I perform the action of..., gratitude is found.

_____

_____

_____

_____

I choose today to...

_____

_____

_____

_____

I feel treasured when...

_____

_____

_____

_____

Date: _____

Now is no time to think of what you do not have. Think of what you can do with what there is.

— ERNEST HEMINGWAY

I will use my resources effectively.

I attract gratitude by doing...

_____

_____

_____

_____

I manifest appreciation when I...

_____

_____

_____

_____

I am having success in...

_____

_____

_____

_____

Date: _____

Have gratitude for the things you're discarding. By giving gratitude, you're giving closure to the relationship with that object, and by doing so, it becomes a lot easier to let go.

— MARIE KONDO

I give thanks and let go.

I am thankful for this one thing...

_____

_____

_____

_____

My joy is found in...

_____

_____

_____

_____

My life improves when I let go of...

_____

_____

_____

_____

Date: _____

*When it comes to life the critical thing
is whether you take things for granted
or take them with gratitude.*

— G.K. CHESTERTON

I value and appreciate everything.

Today, I will not take for granted...

_____

_____

_____

_____

Whenever..., I feel a boost of happiness.

_____

_____

_____

My connection with... is something I value because...

_____

_____

_____

_____

Date: _____

*In counting my blessings,
not my losses, I found joy again.*

— LYNN LOK-PAYNE

Joy is found in a grateful heart.

Focusing on gratitude for... increases my...

_____

_____

_____

_____

It brings me great joy whenever...

_____

_____

_____

Life is better when I act on...

_____

_____

_____

_____

Date: _____

Gratitude is the ability to experience life as a gift. It liberates us from the prison of self-preoccupation.

— JOHN ORTBERG

TODAY'S AFFIRMATION

I'm grateful for my life.

I cultivate appreciation through...

_____

_____

_____

_____

More opportunities come my way when I...

_____

_____

_____

_____

Life is amazing because...

_____

_____

_____

_____

Date: _____

INSPIRATIONAL QUOTE

I cried because I had no shoes,
then I met a man who had no feet.

— MAHATMA GANDHI

I am thankful for what I have.

My objective today is to find thankfulness in...

_____

_____

_____

_____

I am so excited for... to appear in my life.

_____

_____

_____

_____

One thing I appreciate is...

_____

_____

_____

_____

Date: _____

When some things go wrong,
take a moment to be thankful for
the many things that are going right.

— ANNIE GOTTLIER

I concentrate on the positive.

Appreciation grows inside me when I...

_____

_____

_____

_____

Fulfillment gives me an opportunity to...

_____

_____

_____

_____

What's working in my life is...

_____

_____

_____

_____

Date: _____

The secret of being happy is accepting where you are in life and making the most out of every day.

— UNKNOWN

Today's a gift. I'll make it count.

Through..., I cultivate gratitude.

_____

_____

_____

_____

I will redirect my thoughts to better outcomes, like...

_____

_____

_____

_____

One of my favorite activities is...

_____

_____

_____

_____

Date: _____

Every sunset is an opportunity to reset.
Every sunrise begins with new eyes.

— RICHIE NORTON

I can make a new start.

I encourage gratitude by...

_____

_____

_____

_____

Inspiration flows through me when...

_____

_____

_____

_____

My uniqueness comes out when...

_____

_____

_____

_____

Date: _____

Two kinds of gratitude: The sudden kind we feel for what we take; the larger kind we feel for what we give.

— EDWIN ARLINGTON ROBINSON

Giving equals a happy heart.

I am committed to discover the gift of giving by...

_____

_____

_____

_____

My heart is filled with gratitude when I...

_____

_____

_____

_____

I cherish the bond I have with...

_____

_____

_____

_____

Date: _____

Gratitude is the appreciation of things that are not deserved, earned, or demanded – those wonderful things that we take for granted.

— RENÉE PAULE

I'm grateful for the simple things.

I bring in more gratitude when I appreciate...

_____

_____

_____

_____

Appreciation is a power I tap into when I...

_____

_____

_____

_____

I am happy because I have a friend who...

_____

_____

_____

_____

Date: _____

INSPIRATIONAL QUOTE

I choose to find the beauty in this moment.

— LYNN LOK-PAYNE

Today is wonderful day.

My focus today is to explore gratitude in...

_____

_____

_____

_____

Gratitude is expressed by doing...

_____

_____

_____

_____

One thing that stands out to me is...

_____

_____

_____

_____

Date: _____

Gratitude turns what we have into enough.

— ANONYMOUS

I already have everything I need.

I bring appreciation into my life by being thankful for...

_____

_____

_____

_____

I find happiness in...

_____

_____

_____

_____

My strongest quality is...

_____

_____

_____

_____

Date: _____

Gratitude is a powerful catalyst for happiness. It's the spark that lights a fire of joy in your soul.

— AMY COLLETTE

Being grateful increases my joy.

I am dedicated to find gratitude in...

_____

_____

_____

_____

My day is brightened when...

_____

_____

_____

The thing that brings me the greatest joy is...

_____

_____

_____

_____

Date: _____

*Gratitude for the present moment
and the fullness of life now
is the true prosperity.*

— ECKHART TOLLE

I am thankful for right now.

Thankfulness runs through me because I...

_____

_____

_____

_____

Positivity shines when I...

_____

_____

_____

The moments when I feel the most empowered are...

_____

_____

_____

_____

Date: _____

*The greatest source of happiness
is the ability to be grateful at all times.*

— ZIG ZIGLAR

I am grateful for everything.

By..., I bring gratitude in my life.

_____

_____

_____

_____

My source of joy stems from...

_____

_____

_____

_____

The best part of my life is...

_____

_____

_____

_____

Date: _____

*The thankful receiver
bears a plentiful harvest.*

— WILLIAM BLAKE

Thankfulness increases gratitude.

I create appreciation through...

_____

_____

_____

_____

Peace of mind is found in...

_____

_____

_____

My relationship with... brings me...

_____

_____

_____

_____

Date: _____

*What separates privilege
from entitlement is gratitude.*

— BRENÉ BROWN

Gratitude is a great gift.

Today, I actively look for reasons to be grateful for...

_____

_____

_____

_____

When I shift my attention, I find...

_____

_____

_____

_____

When I..., my life gets better.

_____

_____

_____

_____

Date: _____

*Not what we say about our blessings,
but how we use them, is the true measure
of our thanksgiving.*

— W.T. PURKISER

I put my blessings to good use.

When I use my talents, I feel...

_____

_____

_____

_____

My inspiration is amplified when...

_____

_____

_____

_____

My true strength is revealed in...

_____

_____

_____

_____

Date: _____

Let gratitude be your guide to light the way to a life of well-being.

— LYNN LOK-PAYNE

Gratitude guides my life.

I enhance my well-being through...

_____

_____

_____

_____

Gratitude grows when I change my perspective to...

_____

_____

_____

_____

I reach my full potential by being...

_____

_____

_____

_____

Date: _____

*When you express gratitude
for the blessings that come into your life,
it not only encourages the universe
to send you more, it also sees to it
that those blessings remain.*

— STEPHEN RICHARDS

Gratitude attracts abundance.

I become a gratitude magnet whenever I...

_____

_____

_____

_____

I leverage the power of attraction through...

_____

_____

_____

The universe is on my side by supporting me with...

_____

_____

_____

_____

Date: _____

INSPIRATIONAL QUOTE

*There is a calmness to a life lived
in gratitude, a quiet joy.*

— RALPH H. BLUM

Being grateful brings me peace.

I find peace when I...

_____

_____

_____

_____

My spirits are lifted through the act of...

_____

_____

_____

I will... to pursue my joy.

_____

_____

_____

_____

Date: _____

Forget yesterday – it has already forgotten you. Don't sweat tomorrow – you haven't even met. Instead, open your eyes and your heart to a truly precious gift – today.

— STEVE MARABOLI

I embrace the gift of today.

I attract appreciation through...

_____

_____

_____

_____

I feel good when I...

_____

_____

_____

_____

My greatest quality is...

_____

_____

_____

_____

Date: _____

Whatever we are waiting for–
peace of mind, contentment, grace,
the inner awareness of simple abundance–
it will surely come to us, but only when
we are ready to receive it with an open
and grateful heart.

— SARAH BAN BREATHNACH

Gratitude opens my heart.

My mission is to find gratitude in small things, like...

_____

_____

_____

_____

My heart smiles through...

_____

_____

_____

_____

I love the special connection I have with...

_____

_____

_____

_____

Date: _____

I am happy because I'm grateful.
I choose to be grateful. That gratitude
allows me to be happy.

— WILL ARNETT

Joy is found through gratitude.

My appreciation expands through...

_____

_____

_____

_____

Happiness is found whenever I...

_____

_____

_____

_____

Acting on... makes life better.

_____

_____

_____

_____

Date: _____

*There's no happier person than
a truly thankful, content person.*

— JOYCE MEYER

Being thankful makes me happy.

My heart is full whenever I...

_____

_____

_____

_____

The definition of happiness for me is...

_____

_____

_____

_____

I greatly appreciate...

_____

_____

_____

_____

Date: _____

INSPIRATIONAL QUOTE

I'm thankful for my struggle because without it I wouldn't have stumbled across my strength.

— ANONYMOUS

I am thankful for my growth.

Today, I place my attention on personal growth by...

_____

_____

_____

_____

When I..., new opportunities appear.

_____

_____

_____

_____

I feel most empowered by my growth when...

_____

_____

_____

_____

Date: _____

True forgiveness is when you can say,
"Thank you for that experience."

— OPRAH WINFREY

I'm grateful for this experience.

When I..., I identify something to be grateful for.

_____

_____

_____

_____

What inspires me most is...

_____

_____

_____

This unwanted experience helped me to...

_____

_____

_____

_____

Date: _____

Gratitude is a choice. And it is a choice I choose to live in each day.

— LYNN LOK-PAYNE

Choose gratitude.

I am blessed to have...

_____

_____

_____

_____

Today, I choose to...

_____

_____

_____

_____

I am at my best when...

_____

_____

_____

_____

Date: _____

When we give cheerfully and accept gratefully, everyone is blessed.

— MAYA ANGELOU

I give with an open heart.

Giving makes me feel...

_____

_____

_____

_____

Whenever I..., I am uplifted.

_____

_____

_____

_____

The person I treasure is...

_____

_____

_____

_____

Date: _____

Happiness is letting go of what you think your life is supposed to look like and celebrating it for everything that it is.

— MANDY HALE

I celebrate this day.

Today, I celebrate...

_____

_____

_____

_____

I show appreciation through...

_____

_____

_____

_____

My simple joys are...

_____

_____

_____

_____

Date: _____

Gratitude makes sweet miracles of small moments.

— MARY DAVIS

Every single day is a miracle.

Opening my eyes to the wonders around me, I see...

_____

_____

_____

_____

When I change my perspective, I change...

_____

_____

_____

My life is great because of...

_____

_____

_____

_____

Date: _____

*When we focus on our gratitude,
the tide of disappointment goes out
and the tide of love rushes in.*

— KRISTIN ARMSTRONG

Gratitude eases disappointment.

Whenever I..., I find appreciation.

_____

_____

_____

_____

I find my strength when I...

_____

_____

_____

_____

What brings joy to my life is...

_____

_____

_____

_____

Date: _____

Gratitude is not only the greatest of virtues,
but the parent of all others.

— MARCUS TULLIUS CICERO

Gratitude is the ultimate trait.

I live in gratitude when I...

_____

_____

_____

_____

My joy is rooted in...

_____

_____

_____

_____

Happiness follows me because...

_____

_____

_____

_____

Date: _____

*The moment I stopped spending
so much time chasing the big pleasure
of life, I began to enjoy the little ones,
like watching the stars dancing in a
moonlit sky or soaking in the sunbeams
of a glorious summer morning.*

— ROBIN SHARMA

Small pleasures bring great gifts.

Gratitude is easy to find when I focus on...

_____

_____

_____

_____

My happiness cup overflows when...

_____

_____

_____

_____

It's a blessing to have...

_____

_____

_____

_____

Date: _____

Gratitude and kindness exemplify an exceptional life.

— ART RIOS

Kindness reveals thankfulness.

Being thankful helps me to...

_____

_____

_____

_____

I find kindness in...

_____

_____

_____

_____

It's a privilege to know...

_____

_____

_____

_____

Date: _____

The soul that gives thanks can find comfort in everything; the soul that complains can find comfort in nothing.

— HANNAH WHITALL SMITH

Contentment lies in gratitude.

Gratitude flows through me when I focus on...

_____

_____

_____

_____

I feel a sense of fulfillment when...

_____

_____

_____

Life is better when I...

_____

_____

_____

_____

Date: _____

Gratitude is a quality similar to electricity:
It must be produced and discharged
and used up in order to exist at all.

— WILLIAM FAULKNER

Gratitude increases with use.

Appreciation helps me to...

_____

_____

_____

_____

My source of gratitude grows because of...

_____

_____

_____

_____

I fill my life with joy when I...

_____

_____

_____

_____

Date: _____

INSPIRATIONAL QUOTE

*When I started counting my blessings,
my whole life turned around.*

— WILLIE NELSON

Gratitude positively impacts life.

Being thankful creates...

_____

_____

_____

_____

Gratitude grants me the optimism to...

_____

_____

_____

_____

I am in my true authenticity when I...

_____

_____

_____

_____

Date: _____

The more grateful you are, the more you attract things to be thankful for. Let gratitude be your guiding principle and your compass toward a well-lived life.

— LYNN LOK-PAYNE

Gratitude is my inner strength.

Gratitude for... allows me to experience more joy.

_____

_____

_____

_____

My soul is filled with gratitude when I...

_____

_____

_____

_____

The best part of me is...

_____

_____

_____

_____

Date: _____

If the only prayer you ever say in your life is 'thank you,' that would suffice.

— MEISTER ECKHART

Say thank you each and every day.

Today, I give thanks for...

_____

_____

_____

_____

Thank you is my power source for...

_____

_____

_____

_____

I feel lucky for the people in my life because...

_____

_____

_____

_____

Date: _____

And because all things have contributed to your advancement, you should include all things in your gratitude.

— RALPH WALDO EMERSON

I'm grateful for this experience.

This life has given me the wisdom of...

_____

_____

_____

_____

I am grateful for who I have become because...

_____

_____

_____

_____

I wouldn't be where I am today if it wasn't for...

_____

_____

_____

_____

Date: _____

Thank You

I want to express my gratitude to all the readers and personal growth enthusiasts who have been with me throughout this journey. I am forever grateful!

If you enjoyed this journal, please take a few moments to leave a review or star rating on Amazon, Barnes & Noble, Goodreads, or wherever you hang out. I really appreciate it!

AMAZON

BARNES & NOBLE

GOODREADS

About the Author

LYNN LOK-PAYNE is the award-winning author of *Speak This Not That: Positive Affirmations to Have a Better Day* and *Wake Up! Change Up! Rise Up!: Practical Tools for Personal Transformation*, which won the prestigious IBPA Silver Award winner in Self-Help.

As a former CEO and founder of a multi-million-dollar business turned author, Lynn motivates others to become the next chapter of who they are meant to be by creating a more empowering narrative for their life. When not writing, she can be found curled up with a good book, traveling to new locales, and attending concerts.

More from
Lynn Lok-Payne

WELLMINDED
MEDIA

CONNECT ONLINE

Follow @LynnLokPayne

Sign up for weekly emails, tips, and free tools to create a life you love at: LynnLokPayne.com

---

Made in the USA
Columbia, SC
30 August 2024

439c5a0e-4b77-4051-b001-28e0019a0be6R01